Picking Blackberries in a Plague Year

Suz Winspear

Black Pear Press

Picking Blackberries in a Plague Year

First published 2022
by Black Pear Press Limited
www.blackpear.net

Edited by:
Black Pear Press

The moral right of the author has been asserted.

ISBN 978-1-913418-68-7

Cover Design by Black Pear Press

Introduction and Acknowledgements

Many of these poems were written in 2018 and 2019, after my year as Worcestershire Poet Laureate. For me, this was a busy couple of years, filled with live performances, arts festivals, commissions, even performing as a support act for visual/progressive band BABAL at the Marrs Bar in Worcester. I'd barely finished working on one event before it was time to begin preparing for the next—we all had so many exciting plans for 2020!

Then, of course, came the Covid pandemic, and the whole world closed in on itself. It was a new, unfamiliar and worrying time. My plans were gone, and most of my favourite subjects went with them. There were no more people walking home from pubs, and no more solitary late-night strolls through Worcester, enjoying what was going on around me. It was a time to hide away and concentrate on small immediate things; on the seasons, on the natural world, and on a tiny city garden with bad soil. These became the new subjects for my poetry.

With thanks to: Worcestershire LitFest and Fringe, 42Worcester, Worcester City Art Gallery sand Museum, the Canal and River Trust, Karen Langley, Rob Williams, Chris and Jilly Oxlade-Arnott, and to all my friends, both in the physical world and online. We've pulled together and supported one another through difficult times. Things will never be quite the same again—but still, there are always blackberries, a ripe harvest ready for us to pick. We only have to go out and search for them.

Contents

Blackberries

Even in a plague year, there are blackberries.

Even in a plague year, when human plans
are torn apart by circumstance,
when the future is uncertain
and nothing is as we have expected it to be,
there are blackberries.

Even in a plague year, you can take the bag the bread came in,
step into an afternoon of August heat
and search them out, the blackberries,
the bushes heavy with their democratic harvest
to gather, fill the bag, or to eat them where you stand.

Even in a plague year, you can walk through the allotments,
admiring from a distance the fruiting and the flourishing,
the marigolds and mint.
Look inside the greenhouse and wonder at the aubergines,
purple-black and shining in ridiculous abundance.

Even in a plague year, you can pick up from the path
the feather of a crow, admire the blue and silver sheen,
the lightness of its barbs, their delicacy of strength,
remembering old stories of the trickster bird
who left it there where you could find it.

Even in a plague year, there are old brick walls,
over-reached by branches of sweet chestnut trees,
all prickling with sea-urchins, bright and green,
to be cast off in October, across the paving-stones
in time to be picked up for autumn casseroles.

Even in a plague year, there's a gateway on a street

and a cardboard box of apples left outside,
excess crop, surplus to requirements,
and a note in scribbled marker-pen
inviting passers-by to take their fill.

And even in a plague year, there are blackberries—
take what you need, no more, and leave the rest
for the children, birds and foxes who have yet to find them.
No reason to be greedy—hoarded berries only rot.
Leave everyone their share.

For even in a plague year,
or especially in a plague year,
there are blackberries, always blackberries,
with no notion of the plague, just doing what they always do,
just fruiting to the limit of their strength,
those generous blackberries—ripe and asking nothing
from those of us who pick them,
just to eat and thank the growing world
for all that easy harvest, that profusion,
giving so much—they give themselves away
without a second thought, without a grudge.
Yes, even in a plague year there are blackberries.

Bottling the Sky

Inspired by a watercolour by John Ruskin

That single moment,
the brief precise experience
seen for a changing minute—
that one perfect sky.
Nobody else will see it like this,
or feel it like you do.
Pour it into yourself.
It will be gone so quickly.
Fill your eyes,
fill your mind,
and bottle the sky.
Let it mature—
the rarest vintage
to sip from later
held in memory.

This is what I'd Send You

For a friend in the USA

You yearn for rain;
I'd send it if I could—
the change of seasons,
Autumn's rich moist scent
of things done growing,
settling in ripeness
pausing for a moment
in perfect time.
The sweetest fruit comes just before the rot,
pear and damsons on the lips,
blackberries bleeding purple juice
as ghostly toadstools slide at night
from damply loamy soil
and the owl's call gathers darkness in.

Beneath your empty skies
of endless aching Summer,
you yearn for rain.

I'd love to send you Autumn.

Apple Tree

In last night's storm we lost our apple tree.
It churned the earth with broken roots,
crushed roses as it fell.
We never knew the name of the variety—
early, sweet, picked and crunched-on fresh,
cores discarded in the hedge,
a casual and accepted harvest,
a sturdy corner of our garden lives.
Only now we think we should have found a book,
looked it up, researched the apple type,
anchored it with a name.
We should have shown some deserved respect.
No harvests to be gathered-in next year,
just dying wood, heavy on the soil—
too late to speak appreciation now.

Loyal

Birds sense the autumn's approach,
they can feel in their instincts
the shortening days and a chill before dawn.
Swallows and martins line up on the wires by the river,
twitter excitement, a journey before them,
they know they must leave,
travelling out to the warm lands, the strange lands,
across oceans and deserts, away and away.
They'll return. They are loyal.
They'll always come back.
Next spring you will see them again
on the wires by the river
when fresh sunlight splashes the water,
skimming and swooping and back with a shriek of delight,
there'll be swallows and martins again.

There are friends like this too.
They depart, take their journeys
to wherever their instinct might lead them.
They'll be back. They are loyal,
friends to whom I am hefted and bound.
We'll meet on our journeys
though at times we're as distant as planets
but still we come back, we will always come back,
linked by some instinct that means we will meet
at some time or some place
in intertwined threads of lives held together,
beginning again the connection—
we always return.

Conkers

What mind could be so strong
as to walk through green in autumn
beneath horse chestnut trees,
even our poor leaf-blighted city trees,
and not look out for conkers?
I walked that way today
beside the road in autumn sunlight
and my feet crunched spiky roundness.
I had to stop at once,
let free that shine of burning autumn,
fresh richness with a mellow gleam.
Searching round, I found
more conkers, and a dozen more,
then more; I kept on finding them.

I lost all adult dignity.
A child again, I wanted more.
Cars passed—maybe the drivers stared,
but I knew I had to make
yet another bright release.
I filled my bag with that allure,
brought them home,
lined them up on table-tops,
offerings in celebration of autumnal gods.

But they are fading now
with every hour that passes
they turn shabby, brightness fades.
It doesn't last—I know I can't contain the gleam.
I know that by tomorrow morning
they'll be sad brown lumps
filling up the table-space.
Yet for the moment when I hold them
I still see their fading glow.

Grubbing-beast

October, planting flower-bulbs,
I dig the harsh and unforgiving soil,
pull up stones, half-bricks and bottle-tops,
and you are there as always, eyes and beak
and orange-scarlet breast, darting round me,
in between my hands to snatch a squirming mouthful.
Then back up in the hedge, you sing
the autumn song of robins, more complex,
of finer depth and tone than facile summer songs
as though the year's experience
has brought new richness to your voice.

And yet I know, that song
was never meant for me.
You feel the instincts of a distant time
to follow in the wake of grubbing-beasts
and snatch your food from under snouts and hooves
of animals that churn the heavy soil.
Your singing is not meant as my reward
but marks your claim, your property,
a warning call to rival birds
to say, this garden is your own domain
and I am your possession.
I am your own tame grubbing-beast,
poor substitute for aurochs or for boar,
forever digging up this thankless soil
for unknown reasons of my own
(you have no thoughts of next year's daffodils)
a harmless useful grubbing-beast
that pauses in my digging when you sing.
That is what I am to you.

Your prey, if they perceive at all,

will know you as a sharpness
sensed before their end,
whilst I am cataclysm, as my trowel
tears apart dark houses
with the thoughtless devastation
of a wildfire or a flood.

An autumn garden, and the dance
of life and food and death and song,
the way it's been since humans turned the ground
and birds first followed these new beasts.
My digging feeds the robin, kills the worm.
Next spring the daffodils will bloom oblivious,
and in the autumn I will plant some more
and you will sing again to make your claim.
Or if not you, some other robin,
and if not me, some other grubbing-beast.

Night-Scented Catchfly

You wait and sleep throughout the day,
long hours of ordinary sunlight,
comings and goings, busyness,
daytime noise and voices, all that bustle.
You wait until the cars have gone,
until the dogs stop barking.
You stay hidden and ignorable,
tall and green, a weed,
your sticky hairs deterring human touch.
You like to stay private.
Nothing here for daylight folks to see,
you're waiting quietly for the evening.

That is when the dance begins.
A white flower opens
with delicate temptation.
The perfume calls the dancers.
Restrained conductor
of an orchestra of scent
you call them in.
They arrive, the moths in finery,
in velvet, fur and taffeta,
with decorated wings
displaying nightly ballgowns.
They waltz to the intoxication
of perfume's melody.
Dancing through delirium
they give themselves
to this one night,
this single perfect night,
the secret ballroom.

Tomorrow, you will hide away again

until the sunset, when the dance resumes
with other moths.
Beautifully clad, they will have their perfect night
like other moths on other nights,
every night repeated—only the dancers change.
You're a subtle femme fatale—
indulge the splendid season.
Later, your reward will come.
Your seeds will set, and next year
your clever children will conduct another dance.

Magpies

It is good, I think, to share the world
with magpies—
all streetwise glamour,
aristocrat and Jack-the-Lad combined,
strutting with assurance.
They swagger on the lawn,
fly up, an iridescent flash
cackling to the branches.
Not delicate birds, loud and unrefined,
remembering ancestry of predatory dinosaurs.
They're always laughing,
those gaudy airborne pirates,
cheerful plundering opportunists.
They give the garden wildness,
an unpredictability.
Following their own rules,
they're never cute and never pretty,
just cruel and always gorgeous,
always laughing—
magpies.

Artificial Heat

That slow and welcome warmth
on the first winter evening
as the heating is switched on—
the atmosphere fills sullenly
with the scent of summer's gathered dust
burnt away a grain at a time.
The air feels heavy,
sleepy with scorched memories
as light closes in
and a thick brown stew
bubbles on the hob
promising rich flavours,
these drowsy indoor comforts.

Inertia Weeks

The afternoon's grey drizzle arches into evening.
These are the weeks outside time,
between the New Year and the hope of Spring.
Hangover weeks, inertia weeks,
somnolent weeks indoors.

It is hard to think or to feel anything
in the dull endurance of short gloomy days.

I should try to rouse myself,
step out into the world
enter the imagined forest by the hidden gate
to search for forgotten toys in the undergrowth.
I should kneel down to smell the earth,
touch the soil that encloses summer's flowers
hidden in seeds, kept safe from the frost.
But it is January, so all I can do
is sit and watch the grey sky's arch
as the street lights come on early.

I am weighed down by the season.

White Nights

In these complicated summer nights
when the sun sets far too late
and total star-time never comes
we sit up for too many hours
watching the day decay
into pale skies.
It doesn't seem quite real
when the daytime lasts forever.

You and me,
we've often sat up talking such a time
that daylight creeps around the world
and we've gone home
seeking bed and solitude
as the dawn crawls up
and laughs at us.

Denim Sky

Ten o'clock at night
and a pale blue denim sky.
Rustling trees in silhouette
seem anxious in the breeze.
A single gull flies overhead.
Daylight won't let go.

Five nights before the solstice
and yet there are no stars,
and nothing to proclaim the night.
Birds should never sing so late,
I yearn for friendly darkness.

Will I sleep, I wonder?
I wonder—will I sleep?

Underwing

In my living room last night—
late summer night with windows open—
a giant moth, a big red underwing
came in to clatter at the light.
Top wings grey and brown,
below them flashing scarlet
in a fiery enticement that mimicked its desire
as it fought against the lampshade
to immolate itself in electric light,
against the modern icon of a candle,
the indoor flame that hasn't burnt in years.

I caught it in my hands and felt it fight against its rescue
powdering my palms with wing-scales in its struggle,
fighting still to reach the burning light.
I took it to the window,
let it fly out to its natural home,
the world, the quiet darkness of a summer night.
But even with the windows shut
it tried to get back in
wasting its wings against the glass,
its colours falling out in dust
desperate to be scorched by light,
desperate for imagined flame.
Its coloured wings diminished into smoke.

Today I see the window-glass is stained
with dust of grey and brown and scarlet-red,
the splendour beaten out of desperate wings
left colourless.

Ephemeral

I lie down on the grass
still night-tired
with an unresolved hangover.
Standing up or sitting both feel wrong.
I have to lie down where the damp grass
is welcoming against my back
and look up to the blue and white parade—
phoenix, rat, the water-vapour islands,
passing shapes like secret messages
for private interpretation.
And only I am lying here
and only I am seeing them,
giving brief identity
significance
to ephemeral clouds.

Bat-berries

Bats sleep the day away,
the cave roof crammed,
thick and dark as berries,
a harvest of bats
throbbing, trembling in their sleep
dreaming of rich ripe moths
and the perfect velvet night.

The Imagination of Ravens

Ravens see the world as dancing air
above the playground of the land.
To soar, and fall back twisting
through buoyant breeze
and rising thermal strength.
They praise their sky-gods—
sacred breath sustaining ravenkind,
given irrepressible joy of flight.
And then below—
the scavenging and scrimmaging for food
among the land-locked flightless beasts,
coming down to join them, snatch and eat
mocking them in movement,
dark-voiced corvid laughter
then fly again
above the snapping yelps of wolf and fox,
the futile human noise,
back there to dance
among the raven-gods of air,
joyful, unafraid and free.

Heatwave Nocturne

Warm summer night
sitting at my window
I want to sleep but can't
with music spiralling out below
from different places,
houses all restless
with dislocated life
kept up too late for sense—
restless despite the hour.
Rap and Pink Floyd dance together
in urban incongruity.
A car passes.
Someone laughs.
It is far too late to sleep

Digging the New Flowerbed

The soil is thin and dry and sour,
becomes grey dust between my fingers.
Three inches beneath the surface
I find the solid layer
as expected.
It jars as the spade hits it,
the rubble, brick and stones
crammed in so thick the sharpest trowel
can scarcely find a gap between
to reach in and to lever out
another stone, a brick, another more.
I build a heap beside me
of the stones I'm digging out.
They go down deeply.

Someone put them there and rammed them in,
those barriers to roots, to life, to growth,
never thinking somebody
would build a garden in a place like this.
Down on my knees, I prise them out,
each stone and brick a challenge
to my aching slender wrists.
I pull them out and pile them up,
though dizzy in the baking sun.
It grows, that heap of bricks and stones.
I liberate the soil.

I think about the rich brown warmth
of compost I will dig in soon,
the watering to wake it up,
the calm of summer rain,
the mellow leaf mould
carrying the tale of seasons,

autumns, and of rains and rest
that will bring this ground to life.

Next year I hope,
I'll see the flowers here blooming,
with some care, and hope, and cultivation.

City Flowers

I wish that I could somehow find
a country garden rich with loamy soil,
easy to dig, to plant,
where I do not have to fight against
compacted rubble in the sour dry soil.

I dream of that.

But still, my garden grows,
the soil is poor, yet roots reach down
despite the stones and bricks,
somehow finding moisture to survive.
And there are flowers—
maybe they are common city flowers,
nothing fragile, rare or delicate,
they have to fight to thrive round here.
They're tough—
but still they bloom abundantly
and they are beautiful,
these common city flowers.

Ghost-Gardens

No rain for weeks—
the drought torments
the garden and the gardener,
a calling-out for evening duties
when the sun no longer touches leaves,
time for the heavy watering-can.
Piped water, sad substitute for showers
when the grass is cornflake-crunchy underfoot.
The gardener works to keep her plants alive
while the drought contrives to tell an older story.

A camera-drone might spot it,
flying double-house-height over dying lawns—
ghost-gardens, lost elaborate parterres,
grubbed out, forgotten years ago,
the ephemeral art of living things,
the art in time that changes, thrives and dies,
shown now in outline; yellow, brown and green,
lacework of old design, of paths and beds
where owners and admiring guests once walked,
spoke of rare flowers, of herbs and fine design,
where gardeners worked and watered
as now I work and water.
I hope that I might have their sympathy.
I try to keep my plants alive
while the drought reveals ghost-gardens from the past.

Fingernail Moon

Fingernail moon,
the slightest crescent shines
with a perfect manicure.
Below the city's summer sky
that never quite gets dark,
people occupy the streets
fending off bedtime.
I watch them, they ignore me.

An old man walking from the pub
has a greyhound trailing on a leash,
an old dog, but its coat still shines.
It was beautiful once.
Two lads mend a car
as a girl walks past them briskly,
shoes ringing on the pavement,
carrying a quiet cat
in an open basket.
None of them speak or glance another's way,
living in parallel.
Their lives unroll their stories.

A night like this
could be the coincidence of three dramas,
interlocking films.
The sleek dog and the shabby man,
what is their tale?
And they boys with the car,
they switch on a torch, desperate for repair,
in urgent need to be elsewhere quickly.
Then the girl, the basket and the cat,
sharp heels hurrying away,
a story there unfolds

in fragments of experience.
Three stories,
one city street,
one poet
and a fingernail moon.

Residents

A momentary cure for ghosts—
walking out into a mild night,
a night like this,
dazzled by the dance of headlights
safely kerbed, a stream
of concentrating faces behind steering wheels
all of them heading out of town.
Warm voices come up from the pub,
the sounds of sports and beer
and round-faced cheering men in rugby shirts.
Apart from them in so many ways,
still I can enjoy their camaraderie
at a distance—
not my path, but they are happy and benign.
A man walks a dog,
a woman clicks on awkward heels,
and the all-night garage plate-glass windows shine
with tinned baked beans and bags of crisps,
lager cans and cigarettes,
all these late enticements!
At home the books pile up,
e-mails are left unread,
but walking out at night there is no strain,
just streets and passing faces,
so many cars going somewhere else
other lives departing, while the city
empties of its daytime populace.
Only the residents remain.

Fishfingers

A party, late at night
in some stranger's house,
we stood around the grill and watched
fishfingers catching fire,
our bodies needing protein, something
to soak up the inspiration
that was flowing in broken ways,
a shared indifference, unafraid and flying
where the conversation crackled.

We laughed at smoke alarms,
at downstairs neighbours banging on our floor.

Somebody stayed sober.
Someone drove us home.
Somebody woke early to do the daily chores
and wondered what we all found so amusing.

I can't remember who that was.

Long of the Glim

Poem written in a dream, and on waking remembered for long enough for me to write it down . . .

Long of the glim, his mind
draws imaginary connections
between random points.
All night he sits at the window
burning a light alone in the street
to impose fake sense on nonsense,
making fantastical patterns
from mundane chance.
Sometimes he thinks he gets a glimpse
of a world between the worlds
and for a moment he believes
that he can see the meaning
of the universe as it turns.

Handbag

Sitting on dark pavement
underneath the streetlight,
she swears at her phone.
From my window
I hear her angry words.
The light from the screen
illuminates a pretty face.
For the moment she's an actress
in a slice-of-life film.
She might even win an Oscar
and step up to the podium
in an unreal designer gown.

But this is life, not films.

She stands and simply walks away,
discarding behind her
her handbag, her phone, her life,
her entire identity.

Night Journey

You reach a foreign airport late at night,
a white, clean desolate place
of chrome and shiny floors,
no people to be seen.
Disconcerted by the signs
almost understandable in another tongue,
you collect the only suitcase on the carousel.
Then, trusting and passive,
you let a driver you don't know
take you somewhere in a taxi,
along dark roads beyond the airport's glow,
nothing discernible, just night.
Once or twice some headlights pass
illuminating scoops of tarmac,
nothing more.
The landscape that you pass is unrevealed.
You're left unsettled by the unfamiliar billboards
among shuttered houses looking oddly-shaped,
everything a little out-of-place,
recognisable, but still
you know how far from home you really are.

There should have been Snow (Zakopane, Poland)

On the mountains the snow lies heavy,
deep-settled among the mottling rock.
Down here in the town the thaw is well-advanced.
It has come a month early,
leaving ski-slopes stranded for lack of trade.
Grey water swirls in gutters
and an ice-sculpture drips
losing meaning and detail.
A father carries a toboggan
for a disappointed child
as they search together for their melted dream.

Just a Place

Just a place we passed through
on the way to somewhere else.
I saw the village sign,
a pretty name, I thought—
forgotten now.
Houses, broken windows,
empty fields with ungrazed grass
and hedges overgrown,
a barn without a roof.
A man stood hunched in heavy clothes,
standing at a rusted gate,
waiting—I thought he must be waiting.
He turned away. I did not see his face.
The car drove on; I looked back twice.
The first time, he was standing there.
The second, he was gone.

How it Works

The men who built the bridges were ignored
while chaps in top hats got the whole acclaim.
The diggers of the mines were nameless to the world,
squinting at unfamiliar sunlight
with blackened faces, damaged lungs,
though the coal they dug fired factories,
allowed the trains to run and kept the houses warm,
whilst someone else made money.

Always someone does the work, forgotten,
while others get the credit.
Someone has to catch the fish,
someone has to raise the beef,
trudge out in frost and morning cold
to gather in the food for which the chef gets praised.

Regulated

She stands there, weary
wishing she could forget
in an overcoat of damaged lights
and splintered coffee-tables,
furniture
thrown away thirty years ago, lost
except to memory—
Dad's shed, Mum's sewing basket,
her regulated life
everything made or mended,
cut, conserved,
repaired and darned
polished to a stiff perfection.

And as for herself,
she had always dreamed of destruction.

Old Music

In those days, music was a treat,
before the first-made gramophone was wound,
before wax cylinders first turned
to reproduce a creaking scratchy song—
when a ragged band joined in with Sunday hymns
(an organ in the better sort of church)
and in the village pub a fiddler might play,
with dance tunes at the festivals,
at harvest home or on the maypole field.
A music hall in town, a special night,
or concerts saved for, pennies from the wage,
an orchestra heard once a year at most.

Playing solitary piano in their drawing-rooms
only the rich heard music on their own.

The Ghost-cat at the Old Talbot Inn

She sidles out, delicate,
in an insubstantial blur of grey,
insinuates herself mistily
around the legs of bar-stools,
carefully rubs against the ankles
of unsuspecting drinkers.
She miaows with a plaintive voice
that nobody can hear.
Occasionally, some more sensitive might see,
look down and catch their breath
then shrink away.
She stretches her back
for the expected human touch,
the gentle loving stroke
that doesn't come.

Loosestrife

That day they ran with unaccustomed freedom
relishing their strange new lives
distant from the city's typing-pools,
working fields to bring the harvest in
and feed the ration-queues.

Lunchtime in the buzzing wheat-field's heat—
the other girls passed sandwiches around
but Joan and Ruby ran for wooded shade,
the shining brook beneath the trees
edged with purple loosestrife.
They lay down on the cool bank;
their backs pressed down the blooms;
intertwining fingers told a thousand tales,
hair lost all decorum as they kissed.
Later, brushing petals from each other
they swore this day would only be the first,
preserving purple flowers in promise of their lives,
unrationed love, a harvest, sun and cooling shade.
When they went back, untidy, hand in hand,
the other land-girls smiled with silent understanding.

Peace sent them back to towns and offices
with windows shut and rules for tidy dress,
to bomb-sites and to regulated lives,
to parents who expected sons-in-law and prams,
suburban walls and fences, shopping bags.
The letters dwindled, ceased as carpet sweepers
swept the summer sun away
and shade meant just a draught beneath the door.

As Ruby dusts in daily drudgery
a book falls from the shelf and spills

a shower of purple flowers on the floor
each blossom pressed out lifelessly and flat.
She kneels down next to them to see
their colours fading as the kitchen door slams shut.

In the Studio

for Jilly Oxlade-Arnott

Rainy Sunday—
conversation in a quiet studio
that is outside of time.
Clocks and watches do not match
reality as we feel it.
Some people visit,
few of them,
as rain still falls.

In a corner, the artist
silently adds depths
and subtlety to her painting.

September Heatwave

September heatwave
and it feels
like we've been given two days' holiday,
as though we're all returning
uniformed and
dressed for 'back to school'
then told by the headmistress—
term will not begin today.

Tomorrow is a day for sleep,
but now we have a sense of
lack of regulation,
of unexpected release.

This night is free for minds to change.

Outside the continental bar
a row of boys
sit cigaretting on the kerb
feet in the road,
whilst cars crawl slowly past their toes.

Girls in micro-skirts
pour from the warm pub
in a bee-swarm of laughter,
high heels spiking the pavement,
complicating tarmac.

The Marrs Bar throbs
with convivial sound.
Bearers of guitar-cases
arrive to play
and smile at those still waiting at the door.

I think this perfect
free, unsteady
Worcester night will last forever,
or at least until
the clear skies cloud across
and crack into a thunderstorm.

Urbex Photograph

So just what happened here—
tell me the story from what I see
in an empty and forgotten house,
a photo shared on Instagram.

A game of cards interrupted—
dust.
A filmy veil across the winning hand,
nobody has claimed clear victory—
dust.
White wine opened, two glasses,
bottle left unpoured and sour—
dust.

Life is interrupted,
something happened
overlaid with that relentless dust.

I see photographs in frames
smiling faces, maybe family—
dust.
Shoes, a dressing gown
a pair of spectacles—
dust.
A room of hints of broken lives
the story left unfinished,
and always dust—
over chairs and tables,
rugs and shelves and ornaments.

Something stopped
at one particular moment.
Someone later saw it

took pictures,
left footprints in the dust.
I want to know what happened.
I will never know,
just an image in a photograph,
seen on Instagram, scrolled past.
What remains is—
dust.

The Pirate in Retirement

Even here and even now
so far from my beloved sea
I taste the salt upon my lips.
Solid ground feels unsteady
when my muscles flex
for the accustomed roll of the ship.
Buildings fade. Through them
I see horizons, skies
that stretch the world apart
beneath the spreading stars.

I may be wearing land-locked clothes,
windows might enclose the world
to tame the sky with bricks and glass,
but I keep my hidden cutlass bright
whilst my eyes still track the paths of gulls.

Canal Poems

*Written for The Ring Project, organised by the Canal and River Trust,
summer 2018*

1.Beginnings

He was born in noise and dirt,
awakened to shouts and thuds.
The navvies, peacetime armies,
dug him out, fought hard to make him,
to let his regulated water flow.
Many died, but still they fought,
fought against the heavy land on his behalf.
They worked in heat that burned their backs
and cold that froze their fingers
into dead twigs that might snap.
They drank through rowdy nights,
as armies always do,
awoke again to fearful day,
as armies always do.
Working on, they dug his channels
built the bridges and the tunnels
made a gorgeous symmetry of brickwork
in an arch's span of accidental beauty,
whilst engineers designed the locks
and mechanism to maintain
an intricate flow of water.
They oversaw precision
with their calculated planning.

Then when all the tragic work was done,
the battles won by unremembered lives,
the men in top hats stood around
a gold-chained civic mayor with scissors.
His job—to cut a simple satin ribbon

as a brass band played.

From sweat and thought and bones,
from hard work and technology,
the canal was born.
He drew his life from them
his army of fathers.
Only he remembers who they were.

2. Town Canal

The canal hold secrets in his silence,
dark thoughts,
he broods
remembering his past,
accepts his present life,
recalling late night towpaths,
embracing shopping-trolleys
shoes and drinks-cans,
bicycle wheels
given to his water.
He accepts these offerings,
not begrudging
the river's bright accumulation
of shining coins
and broken swords.
Those are her offerings,
and he is her shadow-brother,
dirty, essential and silent
with no expectation of glamour.
He knows his world,
the late night towpath life.
He knows the drinking and the love-making,
the banknotes swapped for powder,
he has seen rough knives,
watched fights.

He keeps his water calm.

The things that humans want to hide
they do by the canal.
Humble and discreet
he keeps their secrets.

3.Salt Barges

Patient at the lock, the barges wait,
broad and low, heavy with Droitwich salt,
dowdier than painted narrowboats,
without the glamour of the Severn Trows
or the red-sailed barges from the Thames,
just quietly doing necessary work.
Not for them the flash of copper kettles,
the dazzle of geranium pots.
Drab and tough, ignored,
they work and are not noticed.
Their departure goes unremarked,
and in their absence
they are not remembered,
except by the canal.

4.Circulation

Hold the thought—
canals and rivers, veins and arteries
circulating life,
pumping through the country, town to town,
industry, prosperity and jobs,
keeping up the balance
in a dizzy dance of trade—
bringing coal and steel to factories,
and all the raw materials they need,
then taking Worcester porcelain, Droitwich salt,

trinkets out of Birmingham,
leather goods from Walsall,
taking them to every town,
right out to the ports to ship to foreign lands—
and bringing back the sugar and the tea
from complicated places,
the fancy goods, exotic wares
to fill the shops with new delights
for workers from the factories to buy.
It circulates, it circulates—
whatever human benefit or cost
the canal supplies his rhythm to the trade.

5.Industrial Canal

Graffiti on the factory wall proclaims
this is the darker side,
the backside of the town.
The canal is quietly listening,
he hears the clunk, the clack of big machines,
the grind of gears, the hammer's thud.
He sees the smear of sooty air
smudging bricks and corrugated iron,
metal mesh protecting glass
of filthy windows.
He is sullen here and gloomy
among the smoke, the fumes
of blackened brick and chimneys.
He holds it all and broods
as he always does, the quiet canal,
shabby, serious and tired.
He knows the rhythm of the day,
the tramp of workers to the factory doors,
the throbbing busy day,
the tramp of workers home,
the complicated noisy nights.

He sees it all,
holds meaning deep.
Polluted, dirty, sullied, watching even so.
Experienced and damaged—
he has seen the world
and yearns to sleep in darkness.

6. Close of Day

It ends, of course it does, the dance of trade.
First trains, then motorways, replace the quiet canal,
quicker than his narrowboats and barges,
service stations speedier than locks,
forgetting old technology.
Factories fall silent, close,
the workers all clock off one final time.
They walk away and nobody comes back.
He misses their footsteps.
He sleeps forgotten, derelict,
out of work like them, unwanted.
Clogged with weeds, his dirty waters make
receptacle for rubbish.
Purposeless,
his smudged and filthy water-ribbon ties
abandoned factories to failing towns
when fish have died and water-birds have gone.
Crumbling bridges drip wet soot.
The mortar falls from brickwork.
And now he sleeps.

7. Canal Reborn

New voices wake him up.
They come, the bright new people.

They come to dredge his water clean,

clear clogged channels
haul out rusted hoards
of trolleys and discarded junk,
restore and scrub the towpaths,
mend the bridges,
letting in the light at last.
The sunlight brings the water back to life.
He wants to sing,
finally set free.
The shadows fall away.

And now the moorhens shriek, their brood of chicks
all melt away to hide in new-sprung reeds
when joggers pass, dog-walkers, folk with bicycles,
people strolling and admiring him,
while the unacknowledged men sit talking,
as they drain the dregs from a beer-can afternoon,
his army of lost fathers all in modern guise.
He sees them and looks over them.

The quiet canal sparkles,
delighted by the wash of painted narrowboats,
the shouts of happy travellers
who marvel at the tunnels, locks,
the gorgeous brickwork of a bygone age,
reflections of the ripples on each gaudy hull.

Once ignored and disregarded
like a shabby uncle at a wedding-feast,
the canal regains his confidence,
sees that all along
he had a beauty of his own.
Awake at last, he knows that he is loved,
but still he remembers all that he has seen,
remembers those who gave him life.
He remembers everything.

51

A Prayer Among the Ruins

Written for Worcester's centenary commemoration of the First World War, November 2018

At the end, at the very end,
after the announcement,
when the final guns fell silent,
we stood and looked about ourselves,
we looked at what we'd made.

We looked at ruins,
the devastated towns, demolished homes,
good farmland churned with blood and poison,
toxins in the soil and woods turned skeletal.
We remembered all the lost and shattered human lives,
on our side or the other,
whichever side we were.

In a broken village, lifeless,
abandoned even by the rats,
its very name obliterated,
we found an ancient church reduced to stones,
some columns, half a wall,
yet the altar still remaining.
One by one, we kneeled.

Some of us prayed there
not knowing if there still might be a God
or if He might be listening.
We made our voiceless prayers
for forgiveness or forgetfulness,
for those for whom we mourned,
for what we had destroyed,
the world we'd lost,

each praying silently, alone,
hoping that we one day might receive
an explanation or atonement,
that there just might be a meaning for all this,
a peaceful world for future generations
to justify our sacrifice,
a better world than this one,
free from hatred and division
with no more war,
above all no more war.

This was our prayer among the ruins.

Mattress

This is what I long for in a mattress—
something like an old-style feather-bed,
something I can fall into,
something warm and welcoming,
yielding to my shape, embracing,
rising up around me in a bundle.
With covers it would make
a comfortable cocoon.
I don't want these hard mattresses
that are good for the posture
that make you lie down straight
like cargo on a wooden shelf—
far too austere!
I want a good soft mattress,
a hammock or a cradle,
where someone I have never known
might sing me lullabies
to help me sleep the restless night away.

Three Trees

Inspired by an engraving by Rembrandt

The moon is just too large tonight
and Venus shines too bright,
but still those three trees stand.
I hardly feel I understand
what's happening tonight,
but still those three trees stand.

Defiant of our world they stand—
their roots tell them a darker, older story,
a story from the Earth.
They understand an ancient way of things.
They watch us, tiny humans,
and from where they stand
the city seems so small.
Elemental, root-bonded to the Earth,
they hold old wisdom
and they watch us
silently.

The Final Speaker

When language fell extinct
poetry was the last to go.
The greetings and the daily words
had no more use with no one left to greet,
no one left for gossip
or to share a friendly chat.
You cannot chat alone.

The final speaker sat outside her hut
as the falling sun glowed tangerine
beneath the gathering clouds.
The air felt heavy, breathless.
She spoke out loud the childhood rhymes
familiar to her inner self,
comforting now, the memories
of a lifetime's poetry.
Nobody who understood remained alive.

The sun set as the final speaker
spoke her final words—
the words of poetry
that were the last to go.

Worcester Lockdown—March 2020

The unlit cinema is dead
to image-hungry eyes;
the pub is shuttered.
I have forgotten to wear a watch.
Among all our cancelled plans
a sort of passionate futility remains.
No one passes underneath my window
coming home from clubs or music-nights.
There is no singing in the street,
no late-night voices.

Tomorrow, of course, the birds at least will sing,
and the springtime is unbroken.

Blackbird

After a sleepless night
of worrying and doubt,
exhausted by my pillows
and the clock's relentless tick,
I met the dawn head-on.
The pale sky faded, softening,
showed starkly delicate boughs and twigs,
the ash tree, furred here and there
by the promise of soft new leaves.
A blackbird sang—I heard him
where the traffic should have been
in the city street, unnaturally silent.
The sky, the branch, the bird, the song.
It could have been a hundred years ago,
or any time at all, on a fine spring morning,
just a simple daily pleasure,
but at that time it felt as though
the moment was meant just for me.
He sang for half an hour
until the morning light grew flat and hard
and the radio, the news
demanded my attention.

Zoom

We meet online, in tiny rectangles.
We talk, perform our poetry and prose
to silent applause,
appreciation muted—
we're at the limits of technology,
an unexpected sound could break the internet.

And we're judging one another's homes,
wondering at backgrounds
and the pictures on the walls.
Afterwards we chat,
speak to familiar faces
that we haven't seen for months
outside these rectangles on screens.

It ends, it switches off
and we're alone again, in silence—
the overwhelming silence.

Love in Lockdown

Nobody will fall in love this year—
no crowded rooms
across which a stranger might be seen,
no nightclub dances,
smooches in the corner,
no chats in bars,
no dates in coffee shops
or anywhere at all—
just a Facebook conversation
or covert lust on Instagram.

At best—
a distanced supermarket glance,
a wave perhaps
then solitary thoughts.
Phone numbers no longer get exchanged.

This year, all kisses must be blown
at a distance.

Walpurgis Night in Lockdown

It's quiet in the city,
unnaturally silent,
feeling later than it is—
inviting in the Other.
Leaves rustle,
lights are switching off.
A heavy mood
as the clocks crawl round to midnight.
Nobody walking out
on this dark night,
leaving an absence,
the freedom for the wilderness
to infiltrate the streets,
reclaim the fragile human realm
for something older, more peculiar.

It happens now—a shout.
Strong men come running out
as a skinny white thing
is racing down Wood Terrace.
Whatever it is,
human or not,
they cannot catch it.

I watch it all, unseen.

Tidy Afternoon

This has been a tidy afternoon,
an afternoon to finish off
the half-uneaten jars that wait
as edible resentments in the fridge,
those olives losing structure,
turning limp in brown liquid,
leftover Christmas pickles
forgotten for half a year,
bought for one solstice, eaten in the next
in a feast of tying up loose ends.
The jars, washed clean at last,
line up on the draining board.
They cannot meet the recycling bin
looking any less than pristine.

This afternoon I washed the dusty lampshade
and the shower-curtain where the mould
had secretly blackened the hem,
working quiet destruction in unseen subtlety
within the humid bathroom gloom.

This afternoon I took some empty picture frames,
cleaned the glass, cut out new mounts
to frame the season's memories,
to finish-off and tidy up
whatever might be left of this strange time
that now must be relinquished.

Resurgence

Written for an outdoor event in July 2021, to begin rebuilding communities again after the Covid pandemic

We became accustomed to indoor solitude
whilst outside the birds sang louder than before.
With traffic gone, the foxes owned the streets
exploring dustbins, scavenging stale sourdough,
banana bread baked for the sake of doing something,
no human company to share it with.
We made nervous supermarket trips,
hands swathed with sanitiser,
waiting in queues for permitted entry.
No one bothered to wear a watch
with hours and days and weeks suspended
in an unreal sun drenched spring and golden summer.
And family proximity sometimes grew too much.
The simple teenage dream of time with friends
discovering selves away from parents' gaze
was sacrificed to kitchen-table classrooms,
all precious aspirations now on screens.

We have all lost so much.

And now, the building back of damaged lives
whilst fearing for the future.
We need to make it better than before.
We need to make it all worthwhile
and focus on a better world,
remembering those times when care-home staff,
who could hold one fragile human hand
when the other scratched the window
towards the tearful daughter on the other side,
were valued more than hedge-fund managers;

when a cleaner who could safely sanitise a room
had higher worth than anybody else;
when staff in shops came out to keep us fed.
Let's honour them now, let's truly value them,
move on from old sad times and open up another world.
Let's do this, all of us together,
make the new world better,
yes, let's make the new world better—
come together—shall we?

But now you stand exhausted, drained
against the window, your silhouette crowned
in gorgeous morning light—a new world on its way,
so much to say, too tired to say it all,
carrying the burden of experience
yearning to let it go,
to find a soft bed in a warm room,
curl up and sleep, release the months of strain.
We've been through this—who knows
what treasure might arise in aftermath,
when we'll welcome in a better
and a wiser generation?

We are tired, but still we try,
we are all trying just to do our best.

Yes please, let's try to do our best.

Epilogue

Theatrical Digs, 1948

With eyes bright from the pantomime sparkle,
from last night's wonder of limelight,
of dancers and laughter, of colour and warmth,
of ponies and girls and amazing adventures,
of virtue rewarded and evil defeated,
of glamour and splendour and hope,
of the Fairy Queen's enchantment—
the landlady's nephew stands in the back yard.

With tears in his eyes, the child sees
the Fairy Queen's tutu pegged-out on the line,
the soap-water dripping on dirty slabs.
The costume is as grey as the heavy sky,
as drab as sooty English brick,
seen in the daylight and stripped of its illusion.

Indoors in the kitchen,
the Fairy Queen herself
in a threadbare dressing-gown,
her hair in netted curlers,
lights another cigarette.

The boy feels disappointment.
In his eyes, last night's magic
has all been washed away.

But the Fairy Queen just smiles.
She knows that once she stands upon the stage
the lights will shine, the music will begin—
then she'll create the magic once again.